FORM
FROM
FORM

KUHL HOUSE POETS

edited by Mark Levine and Emily Wilson

FORM
FROM
FORM

poems by

CHRISTOPHER
BOLIN

University of Iowa Press
Iowa City

University of Iowa Press, Iowa City 52242
Copyright © 2018 by Christopher Bolin
www.uipress.uiowa.edu
Printed in the United States of America

Design by Omega Clay

The University of Iowa Press is a member of Green Press
Initiative and is committed to preserving natural resources.

Printed on acid-free paper

LIBRARY OF CONGRESS CATALOGING-IN-PUBLICATION DATA
Names: Bolin, Christopher, author.
Title: Form from form / by Christopher Bolin.
Description: Iowa City : University of Iowa Press, [2018] |
Series: Kuhl House Poets
Identifiers: LCCN 2018005468 (print) | LCCN 2018007344
(ebook) | ISBN 978-1-60938-605-4 | ISBN 978-1-60938-604-7
(softcover : acid-free paper)
Classification: LCC PS3602.O6533 (ebook) | LCC PS3602.O6533
A6 2018 (print) | DDC 811/.6—dc23
LC record available at https://lccn.loc.gov/2018005468

As always: for Kristin, for Finn

CONTENTS

SECTION I

Tsunami

The netting at the surface of the water
and its three frames of the fisherman's glance
toward whoever called his name;
      and its five frames of his extended arm
and the sixth frame, where his fingernail
or a white petal
his brother dropped
broke free

and his children or his brother's children
working the netting for how many
frames of their father

and the children
pulling vacant frames toward themselves

and his wife
telling his brother's wife, that it was as if
there was a film about the birds
flickering through the frames
that they were making
to remember this world.

Coastal Data

The sudden luminescence of an algae bloom will reverse a seabird's shadow;
                and turn ghost-nets into radar-screens that men will watch

for shapes of men.

    In each of the waves, the coral will hold as briefly as dust blown into colored light;
and the shore and our bodies

                        will be scrimshaw of the sun; and the sun

will be some world's effigy;

and you will never think that it is your world;
or that today

it is not.

Triage Song

This is some of you learning to walk—with your daughters
or with nurses playing your daughters—without annotations of what you say
when you fall. These are the shadows of impressionists' scythes

never shifting
toward the threshers' feet. These are field-guides to the shadows of the drones:

and to their sounds when leaves distort them
and these are the trees

you thought you had raised for the fruit.

These are the pickers' sons you send to warn the others:
this is the open ground they cross and these are their voices
moving at the speed of

the dogs that will not cease barking—and the women who will not
hear them pass.

Film

The delays in the audio will allow the woman in the video not to cry out;
the cut-away shot

       will give the boy a woman's voice, and leave his own
            to call from the crowd

of the next scene: where it is anonymous, and the delays leave the crowd
roaring through the window

       of a distant place: where
the boy's condition

will not be revealed by the doctor, until he is alone in the field

          and it can come

from the sky.

The Circles

The circles

in the snow where the bearers rested the bell
growing concentric

as their bodies weakened; the two pines they
scaled

to suspend the bell between themselves,

bowing
between the third and fourth

handlers
who could not see their counterparts

moving parallel
to them

or smell the smoke in their clothes with
the pines

upon their shoulders, or they might have

asked to relieve them
of their burden and the group might have

dwindled to the four or five of them
who could still imagine

the bell's tolling and

scattering sparrows in the Spring
each time

the trail narrowed and it
announced

blinding branches.

Articles of Faith

It will snow heavily and constantly and you will conceive of the glaciation
                                   of the air. The mountain snows

   will melt and a fountain's cheeks will thicken with minerals. The bits of egg-
shell will hold the scratchings of a predator or the faintest etchings

of a bird ascending toward light.
A sculptor will discover the fossil of a conch, as he works the stone, and will

leave it at the sculpture's lips:
                        and the sculpture will cast a shadow
and the tourists' shadows will gather for its annunciation

                                   of everything to the East.

Crowd Controls

The viewers in the triptych shadows breaking into sequences
of expressions—

        into tableaus

of arriving
a thousand years too late to save them from themselves;

or they are a people
arriving to influence this thought—
clustering

beneath the second panel's sun—and murmuring

        about the bees that brushed their absence

into these
plein-air fields; or they are the people from the hour of video
we reconstruct—

whenever these things
go missing.

Reactivity of Ideas

everyone signaling

    toward the rovers and probes
    we sent to receive ourselves

but from
such a distance

    the aberrations in our signals
    could grow

into
atomic events

we might   send ourselves to mourn
one day

we were in the city and we were calling each other or texting each other and

this is the radiography of the body
and its fillings

punctuating graffiti it passes

and we could be anywhere, when we realize we change its meanings
and have to return

to whichever avenue
reads

kill-
deer birds

Field Initiative 5.1

When the vaccine seemed to sicken them, we left the vials in the sun
to weaken each dose;

    when the messengers relayed new lists we searched for the messengers' names;

along their routes,
    the messengers performed their plays and their roles would never change:
one would be a woman who loved her son

        and the other would play you
        getting your vaccine

        and only you would live
        to speak for her
        and for her son

and everyone loved when you would take her head in your lap
    which is what they would have done if they were you

and everyone loved your description of her son
which reminded them of themselves when they were young

    except that he was stronger
    and faster

and could have played

      either part.

Tandem Lives

Someone synthesized the voices of the sirens
and left them singing

from the spits of land the dredges raised—or someone copied their songs
and sang them in the ports' streets

      where the storefronts accessorized our images
      and anyone could have stolen

from the purses
we appeared to hold

and we might have made a life, here, among the inland factories
and chosen names which were easier to say

to each other
and we could have worked the first shift and

we might have left early, one day, and made it home

before the housings failed
      and the geared shadows caught on the factory walls
and nothing seemed to rise

or fall
that wasn't there.

Manuscript

This is where they tore the vellum

                                  to illuminate the slaughter of the lamb.
And this is where they kept the pages blank

                                          to illuminate the lambs
they did not choose.
This is where they thinned the vellum to illuminate the shroud: and this is

       where pausing

illuminates the absence of the body:
                          which is an illumination of the resurrection
and of the ascension;
and this is the illumination of the second coming:

       of the gold-leafing, smoothing the
                     tufted pages

of the beast.

Litany

I.

The sea-floor volcanoes fusing trash,
           as it passes,

into archipelagoes

         where the birds adapt–

to isolated patterns of themselves or oscillated patterns
of the windblown trash–and to the sealed bottles

distilling water from themselves–and to
raising young

in swales

      of Easter grass;

II.

      the bird-

traps of lost fishermen
made of ballast stones

in the weeks before a bird appears

        when they traced the stones

with light from signal mirrors
and pictured birds' bones

highest
      in the fossil seams.

Low Tide

Containment
crews
looping sonar recordings

of ice-shelves

to keep the whales
from surfacing; with the oil

moving East

and the diving birds casting
themselves

and collecting

as studies for fountains
on shore

where the cliffs rise to the caves
and the caves

reveal

a figure
impaled

where the mineral seep lengthened

the hieroglyph's
horns.

Badlands

They will leave the drills in the last vertical wells and will
strike them with metal scraps

      to disorient themselves;
they will stumble East—to sell the scrap to someone welding

with the blue flames
          of the sulfur seeps;

and he will leave what he welds
beside the flames
         where they will see it, if they pass at night

and nothing will have a name—

         as when the townspeople flee

and he turns the population signs
to add them

to the East.

Blood for Oil

I.

Miles of the empty motions of the oil rigs
              and whatever the workers say to each other
in December

when their breath betrays them: the same apparitions of speech

when they quote their bibles
as when he called for her hands.

II.

She would have known it was the wind brushing sage against the buildings
that she could smell

and she would have known it was a Northern wind;

she would have remembered such buildings from childhood
and seeing every third movement through the missing slats

and how that sped everything
the others

would do.

Homestead

The ranchers cut the wind-belts when they failed
and sold the timber to their neighbors

and each evening:
                   the prairie doubling on the window glass
and the wind amplifying the rattle

and their children wondering
who they will be

              by morning;

——

no one hears the surveyor
                sight the line across their land

but sometimes he lets them peer through the glass
to see where it ends

and his assistant recites a prayer they can read on his lips;

——

the community theaters will adapt the tragedies
for choruses

in antelope masks
and no one will have to sing

when they find her.

Territory

A train traveling West
has flies against its Eastern walls

        and you will feel them when you go to pray; or

you will stand here, as it passes: where the open doors
of the empty cars

        are frames in a film about hunger; and the oil-

spill crews
will salvage what they can

with siphons

        and test the water by bleeding reeds

in widening arcs
until they reach you and you

ask them about the oil-fields and
you tell them the story

they think is about your mother

weaving cardinals into cloth
        whenever wool is stained by blood.

SECTION II

The Restoration Acts

kite-
crippled

birds
at the

edges of
greenways

where the
worm-

wood
pieces

act as
catches

of con-
versations

the
calligrapher

heard
in

foreign
lands

and dia-
grammed

for himself
or

the lover
who had

become anon-
ymous

beneath the
flourish

of his
hands;

Flood Culture

then the first line broke
and the garment district was abandoned to the waves

and the first thread was driven into water
        and the fabric unspooled itself   from the same seam

with the currents loading certain weaves
with others' sequins

            creating tapestries of searchlights
            moving inland

between the towers and the ferris-wheel
loading and unloading

                its buckets of water
and the half-signs at flood-line

along the midway
where the hall of mirrors   extended

the rescuer's hand;

Lake Effect

using the rows
of drying racks:

as looms for fish bone

patterns:
the undulations

of waves

raising and lowering the
cross-

pieces

of each rack
from the boatmen's angles

nearer shore

where the shallow
waves

might

shorten
the threading of the

flukes;

Nation State

fields
with bails

of castoff clothes

bound
in wire grids:

in swatches of

colors
sequencing the future's

flags
with asymmetries

of letters

and
images of fire

flickering

in
future winds

beneath
others' symbols

for

them-
selves;

Inland Motions

the windmill banks
rising from the shoals—from the bolts
at their bases, loosening
by turns of the reflected blades

or the satellite dishes
painted to appear as

windmills on windless days; when
someone is left

scrambling squadrons of jets
to light

the radar room
and your profile

in the pulse of westward turns
and the pilots
over the forests

scanning
the infrared

peoples
for someone who
has been
running: training

tells them
he is
the messenger;

Bills of Lading

workers
    on their hands and knees
articulating fossils

into ascending
toward themselves

    and toward
    cranes' lines still magnetized

from iron work and the crates' nails
loosening

above them
and falling into plaster baths

    and snarling plaster saws
    and

injuring
the dealer's eyes

who works
    left to right

    to where
    bloating

split
the ram's ribs

that no one
sacrificed

for his sight;

Manifest

no moon:
    only the whales' singing echoing   in the ship's open hold

to keep them from falling; only
the story

of their replacements netting the same water
                    with mended nets

and hearing the story, themselves; no moon,

and they laugh
because they know where each other are

      or they cough
      as the darkness composes these things

between them; no moon
and the systems of blocks and tackles

swing the ballast stones
below them

and pin the stowaways against the ship or

drive them to the deck
           where none of them

      is named;

Renderings

we cut graffiti-ed granite from quarry walls
to match the script on the sides of the trains;

we use derailments to signal workers to cross
containment lines; we ship containment tents

inside containment tents; and they work the
guy-lines into the wind: raising tents inside

of tents sealed by chemical drift; and they work
the guy-lines into the ground, sparking the stakes

as they strike them: and the fires are moored
to the windrows the track-layers left or to pallets

burning shapes of un-laid tracks into air and the
satellites model Earth receiving snow and the

stacks of drafts, of watercolors bleed the field-
hands, until the temperature drops;

Pigeon River

Frenchmen use the fur of their coats to scent the snares
and split pemmican among themselves while the oars-
men suck oil from the pemmican rags, with

> François breaking ice along the riverbank
> because someone breaks ice to reach water

and his son mounts the hill with the mapmaker's
pack and its stencils of cities his son has never seen

> and Giroux will not sing for the mapmaker
> but sings, now, and adds the verse about their
> wives

sewing talismans into their clothes; Giroux
does not know François or his son
or that they wear sashes embroidered

> with metal beads, to numb their backs; Giroux
> would not care for the son's lisp or the father's
> checking his hair for lice; Giroux would not care

for the people watching them from the stenciled cities'
windows, or try to draw their faces through the stenciled
lace

but the son cannot forget their expressions
from whenever he gathers the mapmaker's
work, and with Giroux still singing it seems

impossible
that none of them exist;

Water Song

for B. H.

first snow
    and encampments among the colonies
of prairie dogs

to slow the riders;
        first snow and riot gear hanging in the trees
        while they sleep;

first snow and the dogs' muzzles
        tightening with the temperature drop

        and their handlers mistaking their whining
for someone approaching;
first snow
in the tactical plans   for first light;

first snow in the tactical lights
and in the sound cannon   destroying

the subsonic fields
between us;

first snow and the people dragging boughs
to cover their tracks;

first snow
disappearing at the water's edge

or melting in their hair
as they sing; first snow

in reports of never leaving
and in fires on the ridge; first snow

in goods arriving
for the snow;

to scaffold the land

for thought;

Immersion Data

and teams deployed to dye-test the lakes'
high-water marks

      and dye the egrets' legs and egrets' necks
the color of the sky
      to say we lost them in migration or in

migration films;
      and teams to document

the language camps, and the children
in costumes

which would not catch
      on machines, in foreign factories;
      or to document the children

not drowning   to the calling
      of their Christian names;

and teams crossing each lake
to use the islands

as memorials

      of the mainland;

The Silence between Vows

say, *the temple shapes the thought*
to forget the person beside you

     or say, *the people shaped the temple*
from calfskin plans—leached of
blood and hair in scalding baths
whose fires' smoke allowed them views
of what the temple blocked in six months'
time; and the compression of stitches
expanded the temple's scale skyward
against the leather's grain and raised
insets of sanctums and courtyard birds
lured to balance the colors
of courtyard banners
     rising occasionally from the walls
as if in recitation of themselves or wind
when any door opened or anyone kneeled
as if in recitation of what they heard
when the banners' rough cloth worked

the gilding free;

Horse Cult

the ancient architecture shored with dunes
and the deities rough with sand

and limbs and masks and animal herds
carrying sand in relief: to cross

the depthless surfaces and remake themselves
in forms the dunes expand—in constellations

of themselves, spilling from their walls
into herds too vast to lose, and limbs

too quick to cast (for studies of reaching
windward) and our shadows darkening

the limbs and the animals' mouths as they
advance against the surface of the world

or into our imaging of theirs, still bound
to the gods and the veins of glass the lightning

left them

      as legs;

Conduction Figures

overlays of astrological charts
and the likelihood   of being blinded

by their light;
        early spring, and wolf tracks receding
        with the ice

speeding northward
or toward the shade

of shanties
where their disappearance slows

before emptying   midstride,
                into open water;

      and the observers watching the nearer edge
and its tracks filling

as the angle of the sun sinks   a set of claws
into the surface

of the lake,   as if to catch

its own
disturbance;

Single Bullet Myths

the slightest distortion of the lens   by the serial number stamped
into the telescope's steel;

and the sun
tightening the mechanisms of monument weapons; and the clouds

keeping them   from signaling skyward; where bands of lesser
satellites relay squares to city squares

in a sequence that shows them falling
to each other;

or to each other's monument guard   training in the provinces
to ferry plaques between foundries and cities

assigned images
    the guards had stolen

             to cast munitions, themselves;

We Are Never Them

they work the fish-ladder ledges for gold
stripped

from tailings
        channeling the floodplain inland where

there are three studies of thinning
the swallows' eggs

                with caliper marks;

and of

the cornice swallows: of their colonies collapsing
on themselves;

or this is the myth of the enemy
        in the valley, below;

      and the myth   of riding the cornice

to your *enemy's* death;

Form from Form

the circles the helicopters leave in the fields
when the diplomats flee:

their papers moving concentrically   across the grounds:

     revealing cables from capitals
describing the vigils we keep:

or transcribing recordings of dissident songs
unburdening workers

of panels of missiles
thinned in wind-tunnel tests

into the weightless wiring   of the satellites

above the dissident camps
and the reactors scavenged from

medical machines
carried through the streets

     to cast images of their injuries
across

the tourists' film;

The Bridged Distance

and the sun
casts the stencils of ships' names

                          against the shipyard walls:

and the tar on the roofs of the tenements
acts as amber

on the century-old hatches
               of East River barges: and

people capture water's movement
by leaving their prints

on fountain coins:
and the suckling pigs   turn on twine in the windows

and in the windows
         across from them: and someone

is in the afterlife
with

         someone else's god;

SECTION III

Herald

Was it a crater or a sinkhole?

He was fainting when it happened.

And, while it seemed likely he had angered the heavens it was, often,

some collapse of the underworld. Either way,

some measure of the unseen had been taken.

And some students would plaster it,

and publish their findings: *"Preserving vase-shapes—in shifting soil."*

While a few others, spurred by his traces of blood and hair,

would print a pamphlet: *"Earth—*

the weapon used

against the fallen."

Relative-pitch

Horsehair, rooted shallowly, in thought. As he scans the ground—tint of blood.

The snow is calving, from the remnant-drifts, along the lines of shadow. Below the

loose aggregate, of the ridges—the runs of stone sound rain-barrels. He hears them

singing: the deep-throated emptiness: which rises in volume as boulders

disappear from the ridges. And he thinks, he glimpses the emptiness: and his part in

it: in marking the *absence* of each note, with his voice.

Territory

He takes the thing,

inevitably stitched

into the fill of the pincushion,

as the sign of the unborn child.

It was not so long ago, he says,

that it was winter.

And they were a different people.

Any scratching

left furrowed skin.

They went *snow-blind*;

the telephone poles

were their featureless

totems.

Homestead

Trellises testing fields for vines:

raising grapes and morning-glories intermittently through the spring: like

adornments of the arches of a stadium distracting from the struggle,

beyond: and growing ever-so-slowly, *almost illusorily,*

as if painted on velvet-curtains and

brushed upwards:

and yes, losing some of their color, in the process: *and yes,*

exposing him

and his grappling with the others: their intricate holds:

the fireman's cradle.

Horizon

Sparrows on bare branches—as the letters of the seal.

But, from *whom*, arrives, the day?

The hills assume a false-modesty: their human-headed monuments—in blast-powder veils.

Men scaffold the other cliffs—

and drop fabric from the top-most tiers. *To cover the work,*

they say, *for winter.*

Someone ferries mortar up the ladders.

Just enough to lid the eyes, and

keep the heights anonymous.

Merchant

The roots of Japanese Maples wiring the cellar wall: forming these bad connections

with the sky: and with the storms, stabling him here.

He thinks of his Aunt and Uncle surviving a tornado, in the flatlands:

then panning for gold near Pike's Peak, and

striking it, and biting it, with their teeth: taking imprints to identify themselves

should they appear, unrecognizable, in so many fine-robes. Is this

what could happen to him—emerging and owning

all of the land that he sees? With its buckets, of ingots of hail,

to be traded to the bruised.

Staging

I speak pidgin Russian.

But not enough to get to Sochi, for the games.

It would have been hard, if I found a lover on the way.

Of course, the Olympic torch was on *its* way.

(I told you, they were moving Jack Kennedy's grave—and if the footage

overlaps, you'll forgive me.)

I've heard you cannot sleep. Perhaps, I can help.

Imagine struggling in a future life.

You're not as fast or as loved. And your head

is heavier.

An Inheritance of Images

Wind-whipped thickets—lashing,

but for the antler-velvet in the willows.

A trough cutting panes of ice from the absence of a horse.

Small-stones filtering through the piles—occasionally marked as fireflies, by some late-

season count. A company's

name on a burlap-sack tattoos a scarecrow's face.

In which sign should he take comfort—that the resurrection and ascension of the body

will occur? These *arrows* pin-

ning half-feathers to the dead?

Flying Dream

Empty electrodes:

lily pads, without a swimmer—to brush and quicken

(until they ready him, and rig him up). And he wonders (as they're connecting him)

if *they* have nightmares? If,

after working with heart-paddles for hours, they look down, and find

salad-spoons in their hands?

That must be it, he decides. Why they are always double-

checking their hands:

why they are double-gloved and using long-handled tools: why

the heart needs to beat on its own.

Recovery

There are dog bites on each of the dog's archetypes—though

the punctures grow shallow over time.

All of the birds, near all of the fires, are red-breasted and black-

backed.

You look like him when you are smiling. This calms the dog.

It need only think one thing.

The infirmary is on the top floor.

But it really doesn't matter.

How close to the sun is sterile, depends on who checks.

Appointed Hour

By dusk: the sun breaches the house–and leaves everything exposed:

the flypaper *develops*–and moves by power of the few, free wings.

The universe is repeating, nearer and nearer the observer:

the cosmos–and all of its solar eclipses: *the dark horses*–with the rings of

their harnesses gleaming: affording after-light to their passersby: to the half-phase

of their expressions: leaving *us* to divine the half-headed grooms, from the others:

by the split-fruit, in their hands.

Sabbath

To sleep on straw-beds. To let it pierce the covers like fresh-growth. And harvest it

for a child's head. What comfort is the Lord, who giveth and taketh away? If some-

one chafes the bell-rope: smooth it with your hands. Peer through the hole in the ceil-

ing. Note the bowl of the bell. Shake the last, hardened drop against its sides. Glance

through the windows in the doors. Behold the crop-circles of heavy-headed meal. The

concussions.

Loneliness of the Made World

Contemplatives reverse their window-screens to pollinate their plants:

a higher floor could not raise violets (though they take an hour

on the grounds and catch things in their clothes).

He considers the progress of the landfill.

He considers the rain—forming its layers of papier-mâché

and casting the scavengers' feet. And he longs for the day

when everything refers to itself—as when Christ's singing made canticles

of every song.

Echo-location

He always hears back

and senses the world is small–*atomic*.

Fruit-trees are weathering the floods in pairs. And today's buds

(of blackbird young) are unfurling (each graft failing

at first-light).

Future-beings: your food-drops *are coming*. So, too, your rations of leaflets.

And the small encouragements of relativity:

none of you is hungrier than the other: the

caged bats are stuffed with grids.

Immersion

Columns of roiling marble: funneling heavenward—

loading their cornices of sculpted stone;

making everyone bow their heads

and leaving them staring,

at the flecked-marble flooring,

like silt-blind fish. His rash

is migrating toward the sweetness of his breath:

the last of this horde, afflicting him, is *winged*

with dry-skin. The preacher is preaching about the end of the world.

Everyone fits on the crying-room window.

SECTION IV

Accumulations

They used the obsidian
        flaking into the wind

to down these birds

or scattered rocks on frozen lakes
to stone fish

each Spring;
        later, they hung panes of glass
in the flyway

trees;

and the birders' blinds
spread across preserves:

the drawings on their fabric walls
made crude by gusts

shifting them
and sharpening beaks or bleeding

the colored bands
across their backs

and the birds that are injured
will be cut

from the walls

for study
and their fibers put on slides

                    to check for any

errant
threads

of sky

Boundary Forest

The disturbance
of the snares

in the evergreen rows:
loose

needles
making pointillist

renderings
of the things we will

never see;
at night,

the distant motion-

cameras' flashes—
the anonymous

sounding
of those lights; and no one
naming

whatever is born

under this
constellation

of animal flight.

Emigration Song

When everyone
leaves,

the plane
shadow

forms an ice-
bridge

and no one
can hear

themselves

crossing
and no one can

hear

themselves
staying

and

we are
one people

still

missing
from

other lands.

Simulations of Spring

I.

salt-lines advancing, from shore roads,
      in the shapes of the lakes, themselves,

or in the contours of an animal's heart
contracting

too slowly,   to scavenge the fish
the myth says

     the remnant ice delivers—*half*-kept—
to believers

     who split the fish along their spines

which pierce
or never pierce the animal's belly

as they sing or never sing
     to cover its cries;

II.

we run conduction tests
     on the graphite shores

and find traces of amperage in stray marks
and in wading birds warmed

by the current–
and in others'

      whose feathers'
      filaments

clench
   the beast's jaw.

Regional Shadow

the latitudes the arctic
became ambient
and the scientists primed stainless steel

with breath-made images
of the rising and falling
of ice

and the silence the deckhands observed
seemed less
and less personal

and the water was the whale-breached water
of the seventh day
until it was the water
of another day

and no one made claims
with any emblem of themselves or their
country

to magnetic fields
or to castoff metals
drawing ice-

shelves into ice-shelves
or the station frames
repeating

their emptiness
across the intervals

of past routes

Sound Mills

        from stalk to stalk the static built in the locusts' mouths
and the fields they burned were studies of the fields they burned

the day before
when they struck the wire

        strung between the fields and the same note

marked their passing
and you knew no snow had slackened it;

you could catch their legs in certain weaves of scarecrows' shirts
and save nothing for yourselves

        you could hum the wire's note because you knew it and they were
passing back and forth between your thoughts

you could walk the hedgerows and windbreaks for the neighbors' clothes
and you could dress yourself

        as someone they would know or as someone they would
    pretend to know

for news of winter wheat; you could tell them of the Lord and of the coming
of the end

       or of freighters
laden with pallets of bills moving toward both coasts and of the snow

        that bleeds the ink through their slats
        into renderings

of their emptied forms.

Simulations of Never Being Born

Fingerprints in anonymous paintings:
details

in the coiling of the snake your father cut
                                   with a garden spade
while your mother waited to be mentioned

                    and could only give birth

because the snake had been killed
                         on the steps
while the priest stayed with them

who might have let it live just
to go unmentioned

          and let us not call him *Father* and confuse them as
          just now,
                    your mother has not yet heard
          your father's steps

and the leaves are not yet flaring
with the spade's sparks

and she has not yet
          opened the door
inward

and drawn the smoke
          against her legs.

Labor

Without access to workers,

    we collected window screens from company towns; we
collected miners' lamps

from constellations in coal-seams—
               or loose stones from the breath-
               strafed barriers

between us;
we collected hatches from air-shafts

and compared their markings or no markings on the metal or the wood; our

detonation teams
       unleashed detection dogs and their frozen forms
brought them forward

one by one,
with commands

      echoing
      in their blast suits.

January Studies

Nurses using surgical lights
        to dry their patients' lips
or to cast their profiles

     on linens,
for the students to practice their stitches,
        who are bound to
pucker them and part
     the shadow's lips

     as if to shift the silence

Eastward
     to hear the birds' first calls

over the straits
where sailors make notes in the sails
        of their sketches

of the numbers of flares
they launch

     to unburden the planes

of ice.

Intercession Myth

Holding the snakes' sloughed skins
                and letting the rattles' bulbs

distort his fingers: how else
would you find these splinters,

you wonder, and
you remember   that in the hymn, the saints' steps

synchronize themselves and no one
reaches the Lord,

first–the name you might have heard
       is never uttered–

and you tell the boy to listen to your voice
and he asks if you had

hung their skins in these junipers,
              would the rattles' bulbs

increase
the raven's size?

Acuity of Evening

The record of the imperfection of your thoughts
before they administer

anesthetic;
     or the anonymity of the crowds in your prayers

and of choosing a balcony to the side of their surges, and

whoever turns
to convince you, you are praying for yourself

     and you, unable to move

     as if the balcony did not have a room behind it
in which everything you remember

is revealed
by the stent

     funneling surgical light
     into the shadow of the surgeon's hand.

Fire-lines

How many excavations of brick-
kilns

              have we mistaken for foundations

of temples?—and how many priests
would they have housed?—and would they have blessed the bridges

the masons would have built?—*the blessings slowing some traveler*

who could not have known there would be a bridge
or that he would not

need
       the ferryman's name;

and if it isn't raining
none of them will see his ribs through his shirt

and split their alms
for his days-long journey toward the cities
                 with the songs growing shorter

as the birds' breasts
are tightened

by
smoke.

Fault-lines

Slings
the planes used to gather water
                              abandoned when they tore—

left floating among the un-
rescued whales

                    cresting in the firelight—
                              among trawlers
set adrift

by their crews
so their cranes might work the recovery scenes

and raise the recovery grids
against

            the sky

at dawn
when men cluster

            and the shipyard shadows
            reenact

everything shifting
toward the

sea.

Amplification Industry

the cylinders of bore-tests
speeding the half-lives of
artifacts—

      or the tilt of a centrifuge
      at altitude

and the pitch of its spinning
in its slipstream

or in the slipstreams of cylinders
angling, together—   and

the trays of bore-test bone
oriented by tooth-marks

to a single mouth

      and the cylinders giving the ear-
bones
something to strike—with each

revolution
speeding the half-life

of *which*
worker's silence?

94

Earthbound

Raining and the water shifting
                        color against the sediment-
banded hills—

      and the fires
      set to harden the overhangs—
and the fires

set in blue-earth caves
to fix the sky for planting—

                    have all gone out;
the river swelling and flushing the sulfur pools

the antelope used
to cover their scent; fields of space-

debris
distorting spectrums of failing stars in instruments

isolating
their disappearances

              from our own.

Almanac

When there was no grain,
they relied on the sun

to tighten the silo's rivets—

     in short blasts—
and daze the pigeons;

         when the emptiness of the horizons
was not the grain-worn emptiness

of August;

when sheet-metal strips
tented in the sun,

in the fields—

     and they used them to blind themselves
and told themselves

they were signaling someone

they remembered;
and when

no one came

to guide them
back.

Third Prefecture

Symptom-recognition software sifting through the video
    and emissaries from outbreak teams

offering instructions for living our lives;

    and if they ask you why you serve them tea, tell them
    it fogs their masks, tell them it is a custom

that slows their census;
if they ask you why you never look them in the eye, ask them

to turn off their headlamps; tell them

you remember the sun pulsing between buildings you passed
    and that it raised your dominant hand

tell them it blazed for the woman beside you;
tell them you think you were one of them;
        and if they ask you to open your eyes,

    tell them
the field-guides to luminescent things

        light themselves.

Acknowledgments

Grateful acknowledgment is given to the MacDowell Colony and the Corporation of Yaddo for time and space to complete this book. Thank you to Mark Levine and Emily Wilson, whose keen eyes and generous spirits tended to these poems. And thank you to the following journals for publishing parts of this collection: "Tsunami" in the *Colorado Review*; "Manuscript" in *Prairie Schooner*; "Acuity of Evening" in the *Elephants*; "Immersion Data" in *Anomaly*; "January Studies" in the *North American Review*; "Badlands" and "Litany" in *Hyperallergic*; and "Coastal Data" and "Earthbound" in *Conduit*.

KUHL HOUSE POETS

Christopher Bolin
Ascension Theory

Christopher Bolin
Form from Form

Shane Book
Congotronic

Oni Buchanan
Must a Violence

Michele Glazer
*On Tact, & the Made Up
   World*

David Micah Greenberg
Planned Solstice

Jeff Griffin
Lost and

John Isles
Ark

John Isles
Inverse Sky

Aaron McCollough
Rank

Randall Potts
Trickster

Bin Ramke
Airs, Waters, Places

Bin Ramke
Matter

Michelle Robinson
The Life of a Hunter

Vanessa Roveto
bodys

Robyn Schiff
Revolver

Robyn Schiff
Worth

Sarah V. Schweig
Take Nothing with You

Rod Smith
Deed

Donna Stonecipher
Transaction Histories

Cole Swensen
*The Book of a Hundred
   Hands*

Cole Swensen
Such Rich Hour

Tony Tost
Complex Sleep

Pimone Triplett
Supply Chain

Nick Twemlow
*Attributed to the
   Harrow Painter*

Susan Wheeler
Meme

Emily Wilson
The Keep